Edwards
grapnel
Ellis
mushroom
Trotman
martin
Mooring
Byers
Hall's
Rodgers

Edwards
Grapnel
Ellis
mushroom
Trotman
martin
Byers
Rodgers
Hall's
Rodgers
James

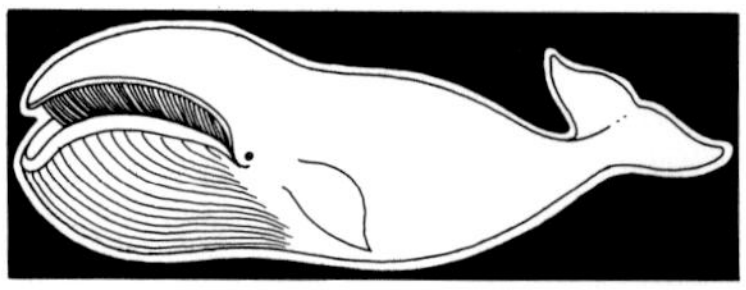

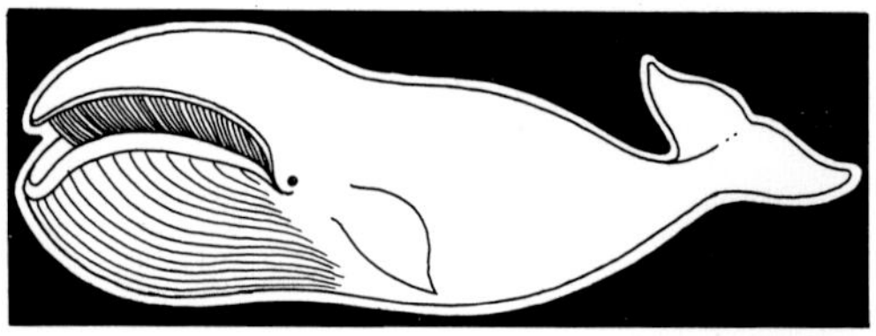

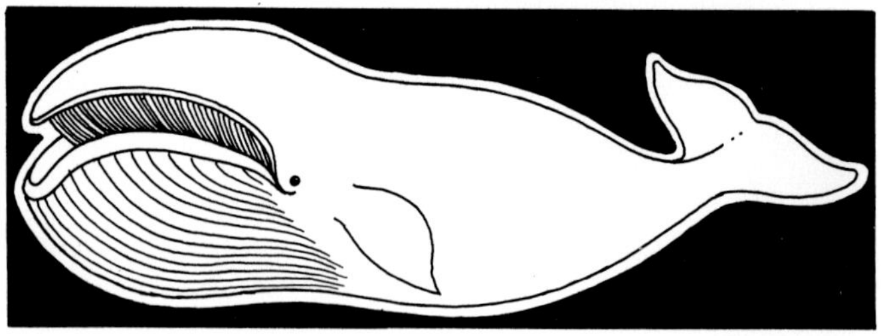

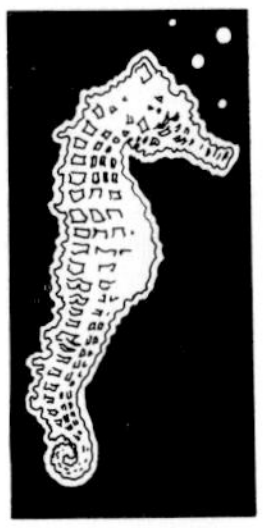

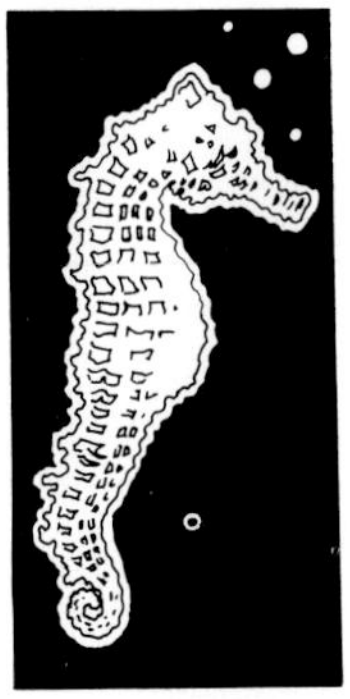

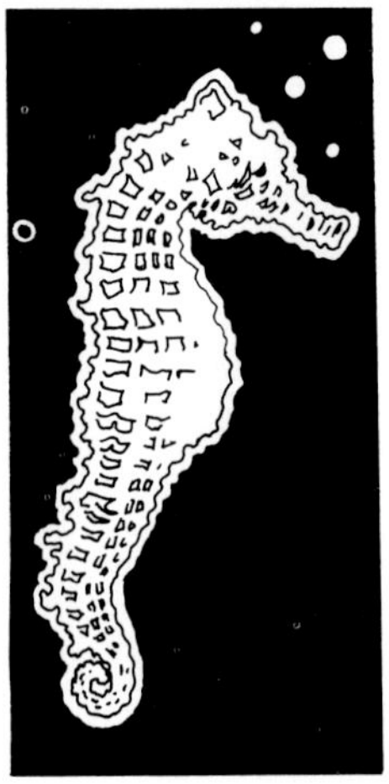

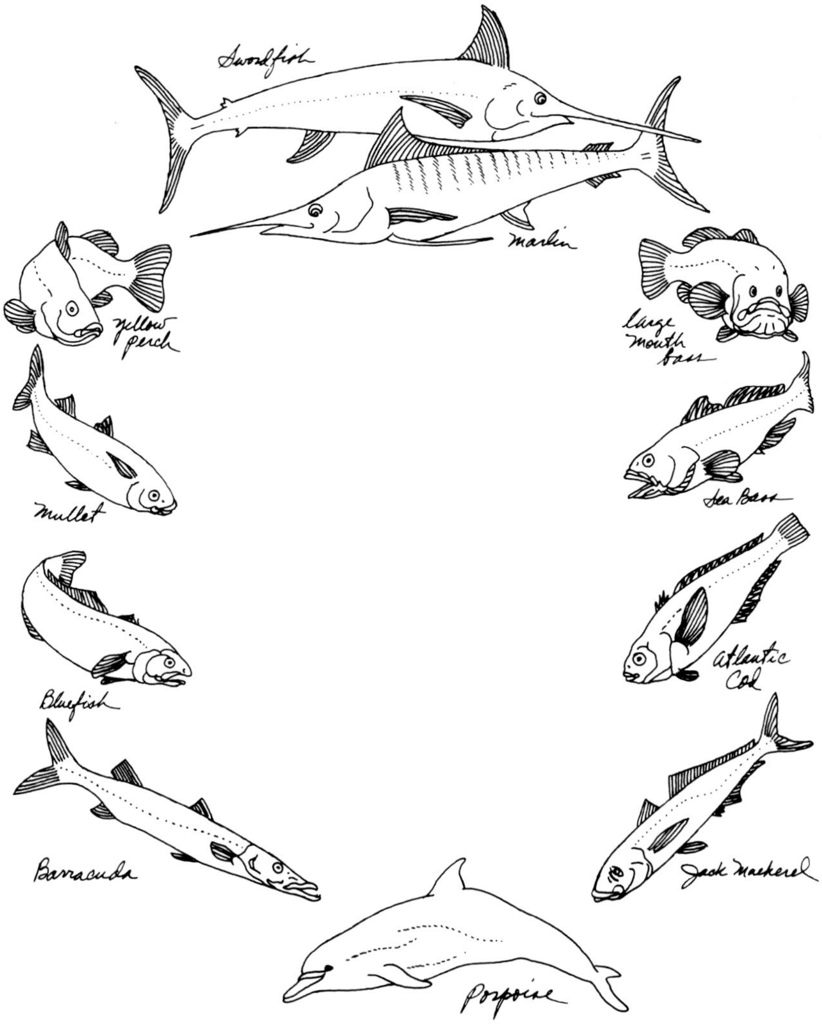
Swordfish
Marlin
Yellow perch
Large mouth bass
Mullet
Sea Bass
Bluefish
Atlantic Cod
Barracuda
Jack Mackerel
Porpoise

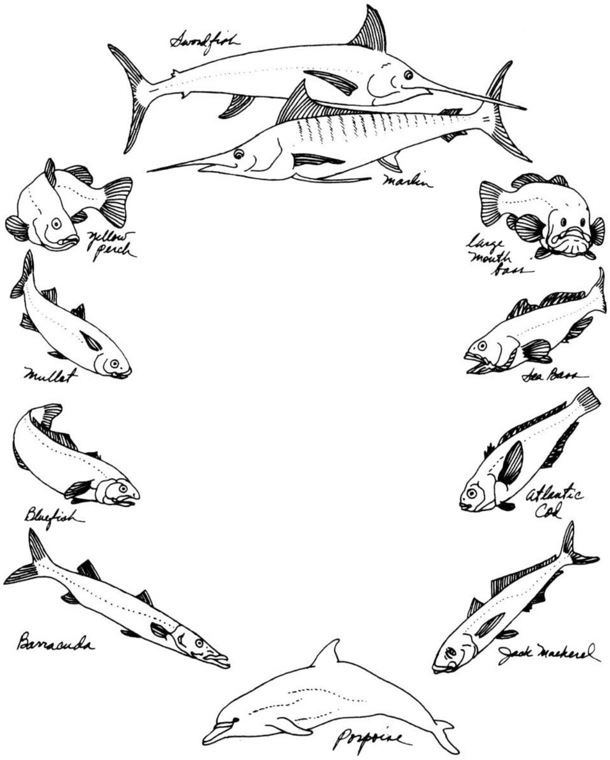
Swordfish
Marlin
Yellow perch
Large mouth bass
Mullet
Sea Bass
Bluefish
Atlantic Cod
Barracuda
Jack Mackerel
Porpoise

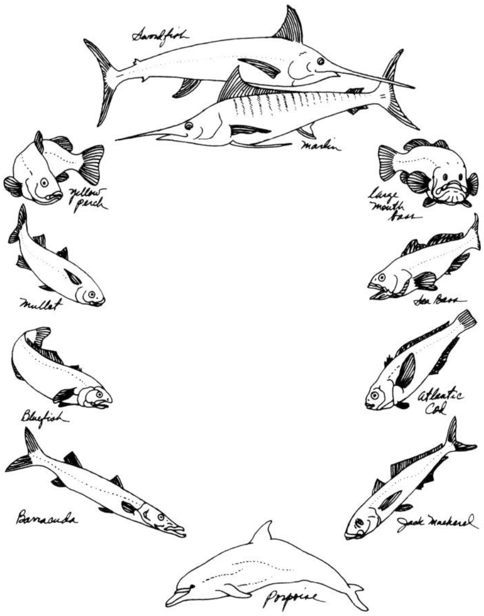
Swordfish
Marlin
Yellow perch
Large mouth bass
Mullet
Sea Bass
Bluefish
Atlantic Cod
Barracuda
Jack Mackerel
Porpoise

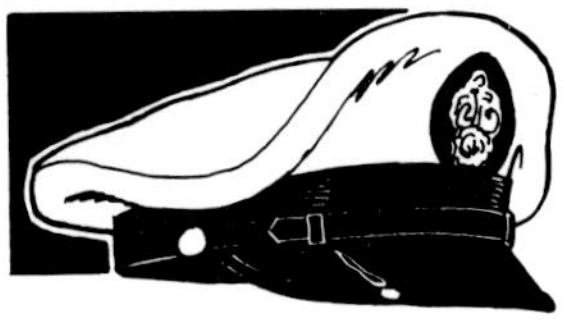

A.
B.
C.
D
E.
F
G
Z
H
Y
I
X
J
W
K
V
L
U
M
T
S
R
Q
P
O
N

A.
B.
C
D
E.
F
G
H
I
J
K
L
M
N
O
P
Q
R
S
T
U
V
W
X
Y
Z

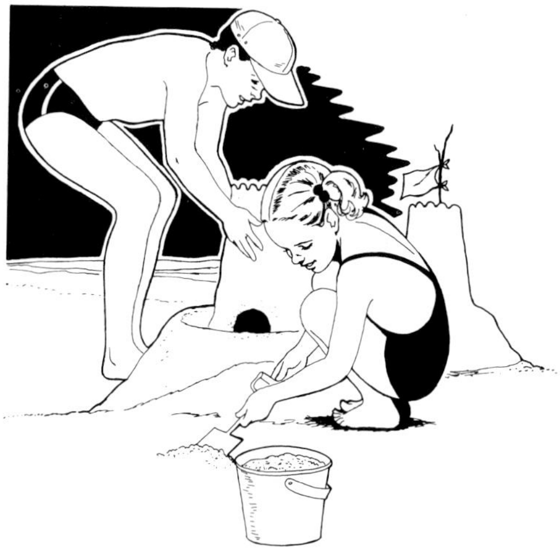

MUSTARD

MUSTARD

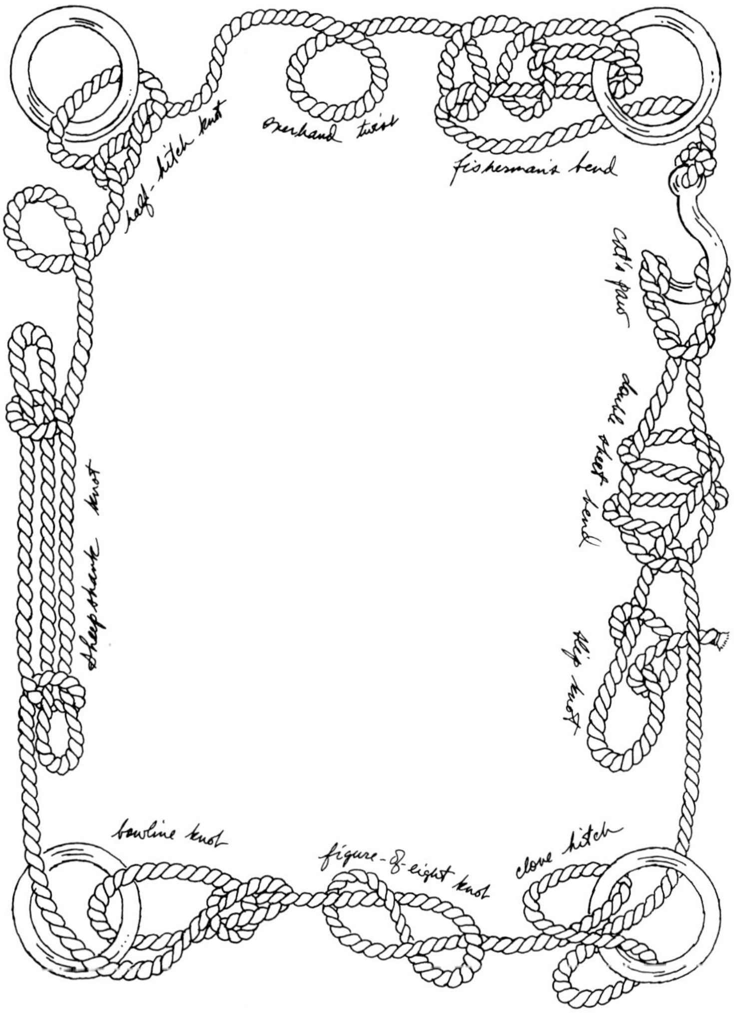
half-hitch knot
overhand twist
fisherman's bend
cat's paw
double sheet bend
slip knot
sheepshank knot
bowline knot
figure-of-eight knot
clove hitch

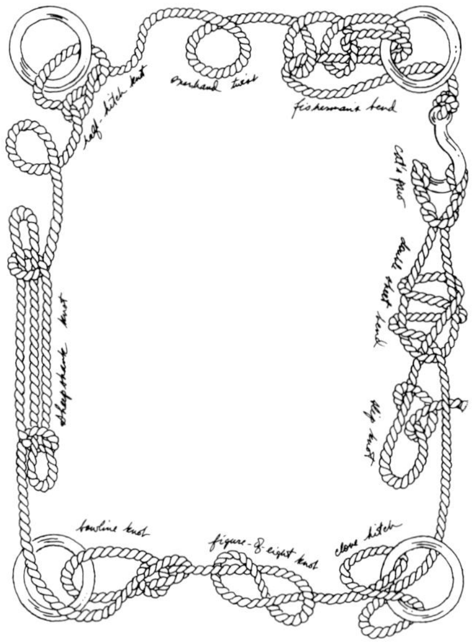
half-hitch knot
overhand twist
fisherman's bend
cat's paw
double sheet bend
slip knot
sheepshank knot
bowline knot
figure-of-eight knot
clove hitch

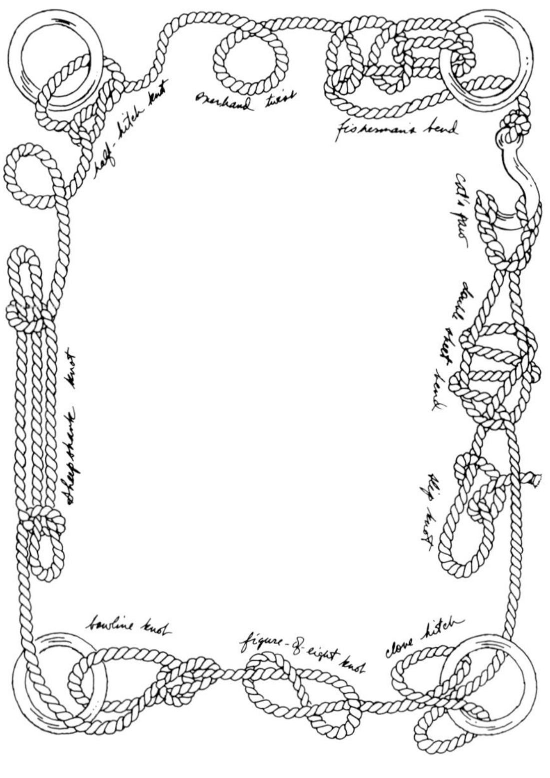
half-hitch knot
overhand twist
fisherman's bend
cat's paw
double sheet bend
slip knot
sheepshank knot
bowline knot
figure-of-eight knot
clove hitch

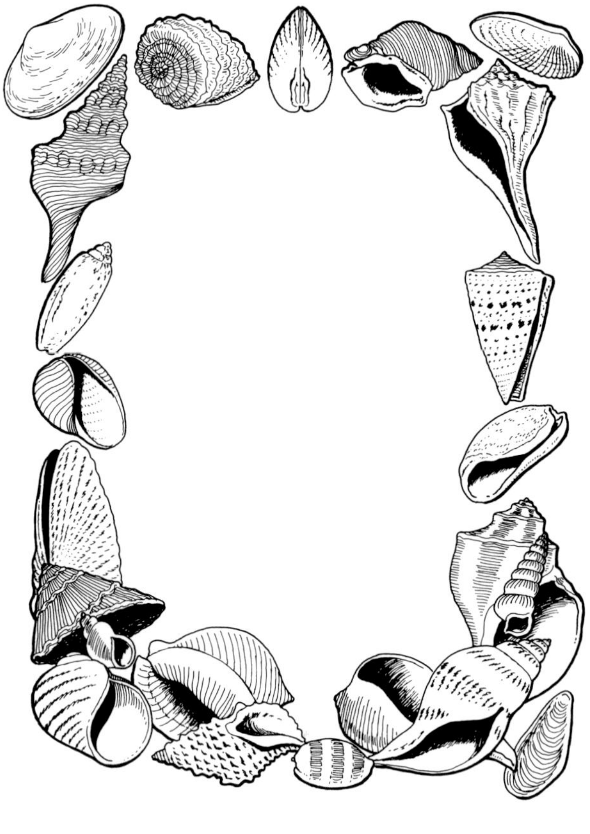

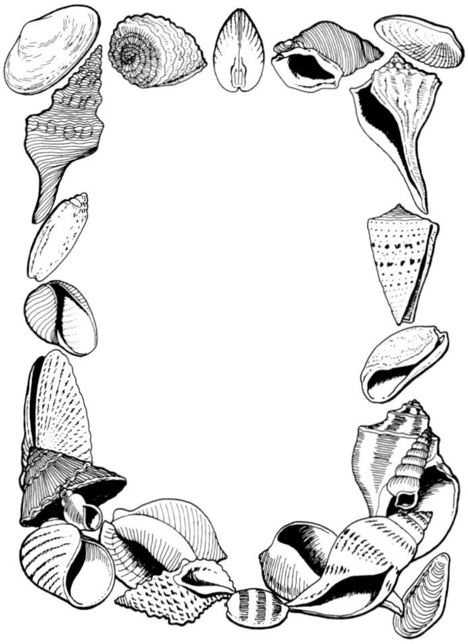

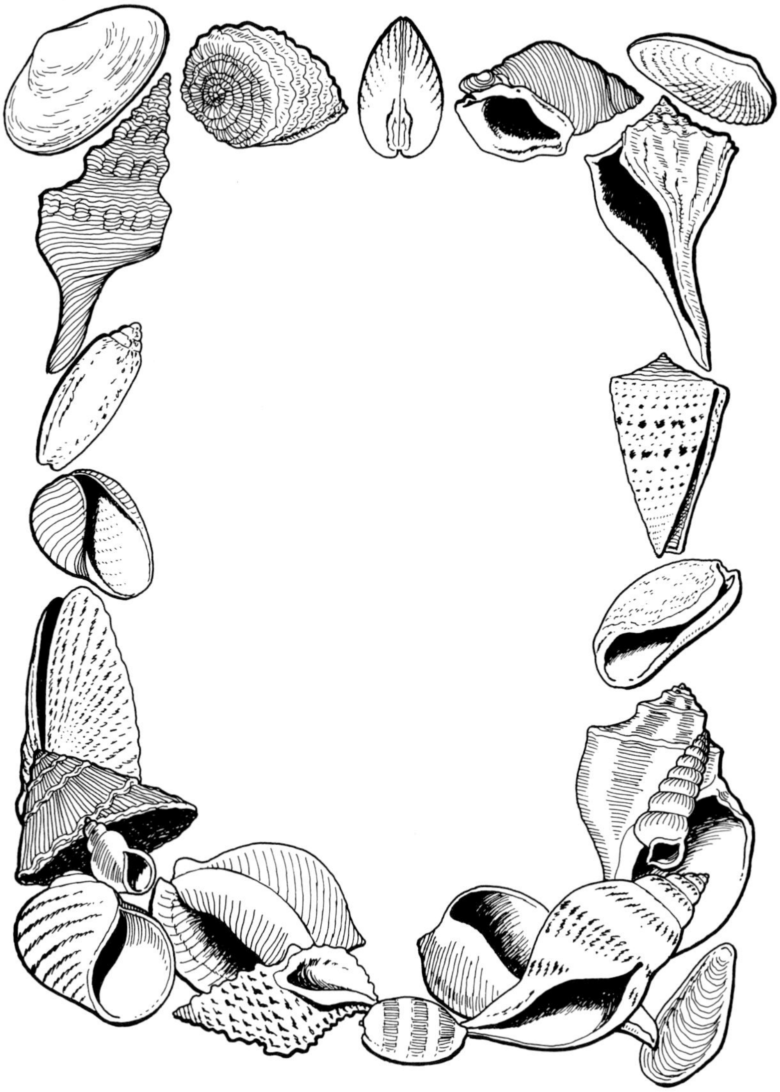

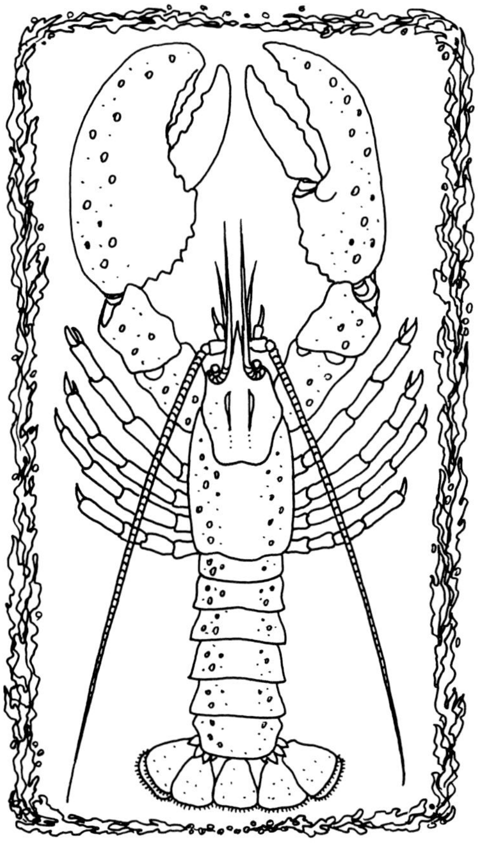

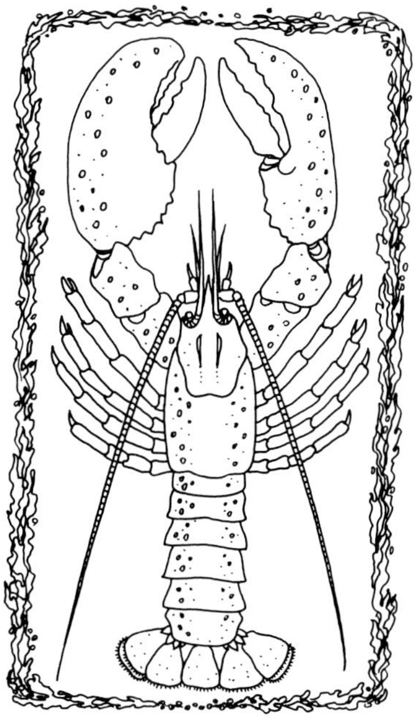

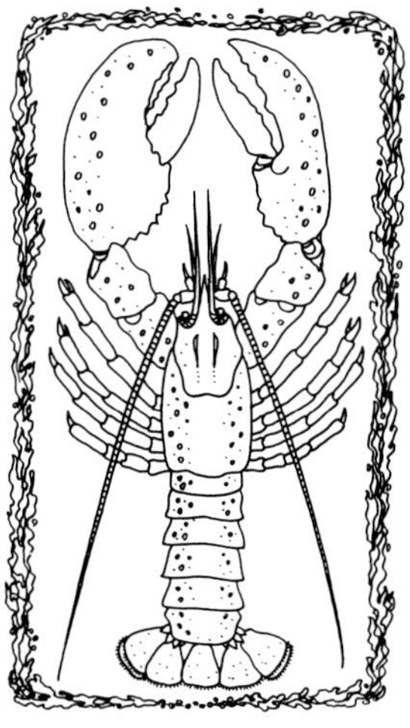

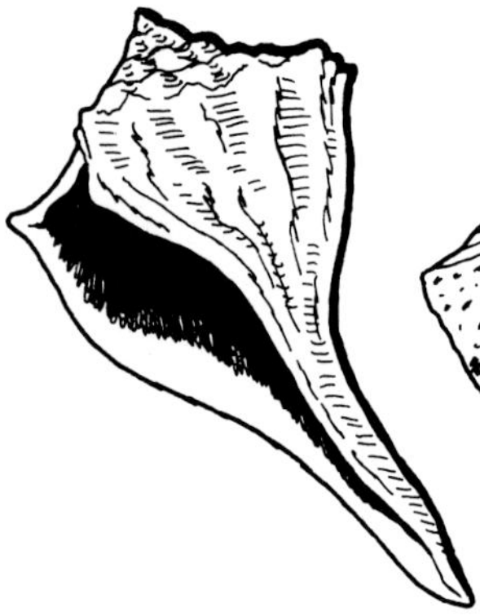
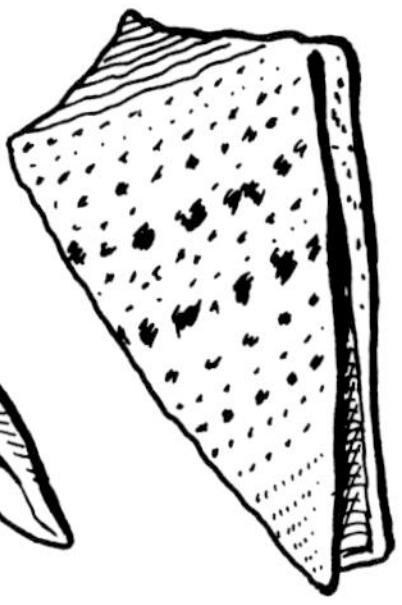

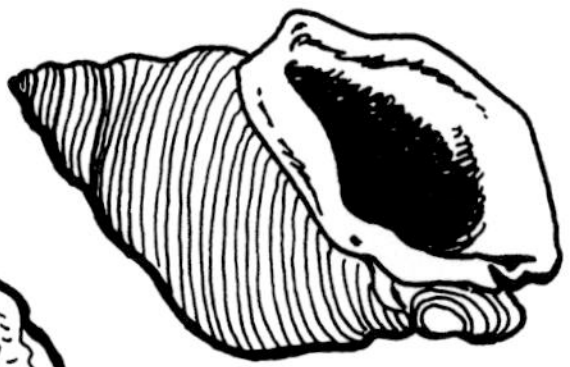

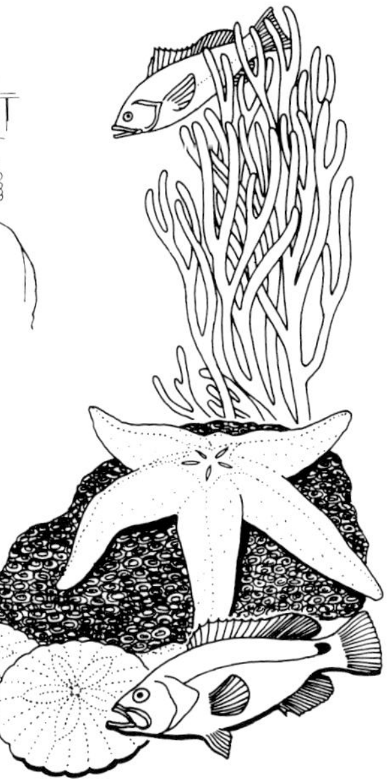

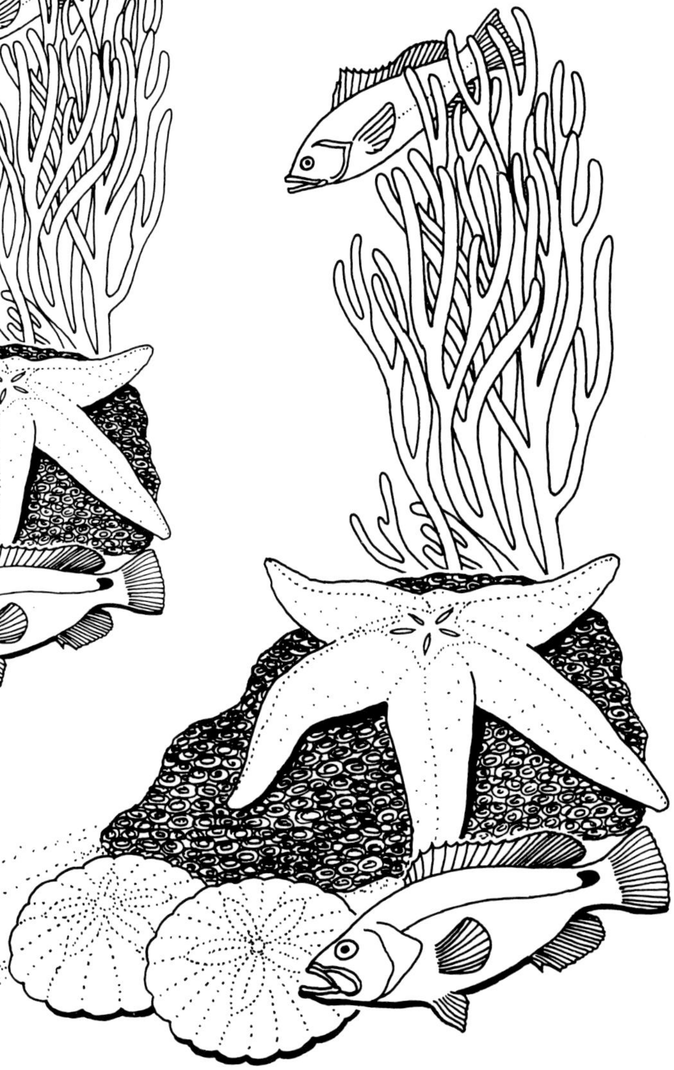

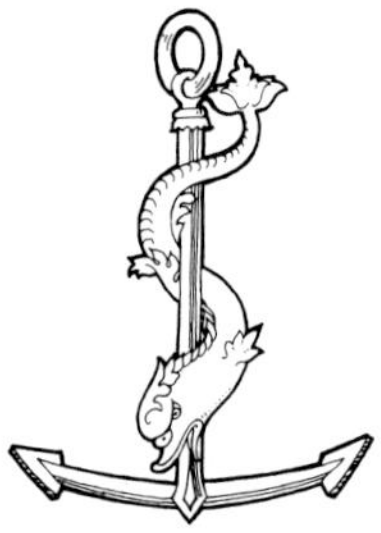
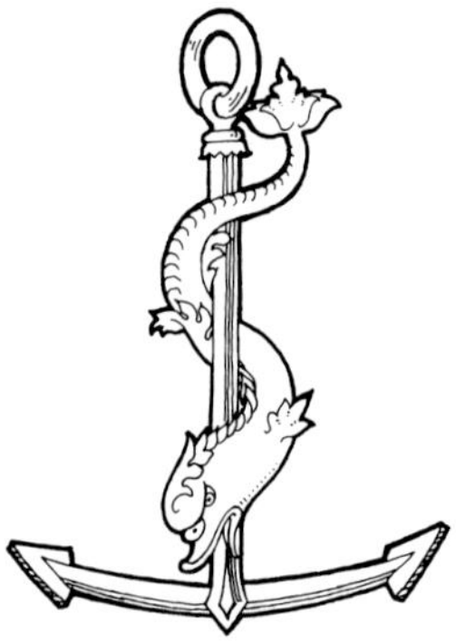
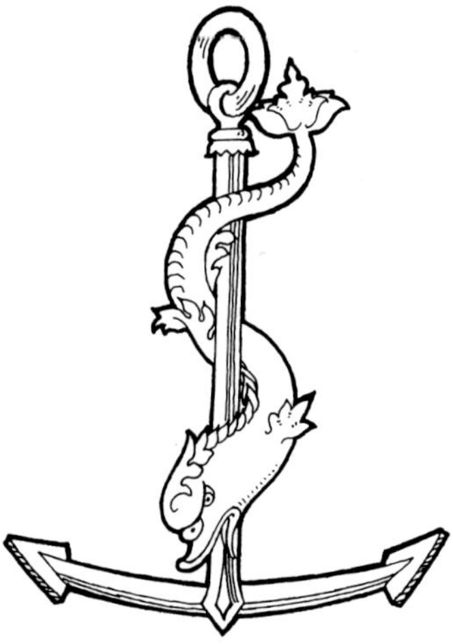

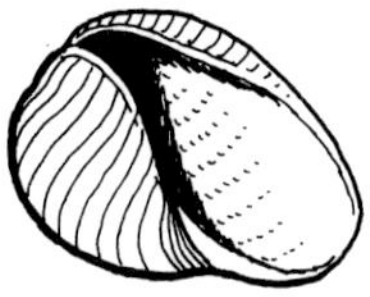
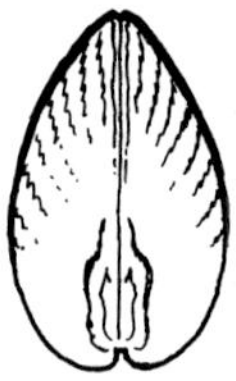
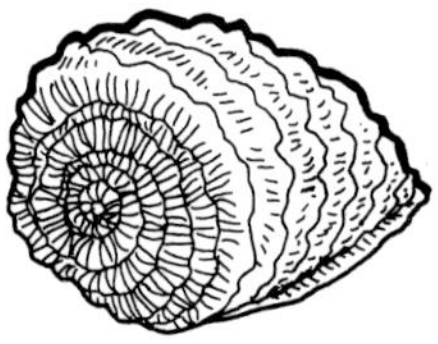
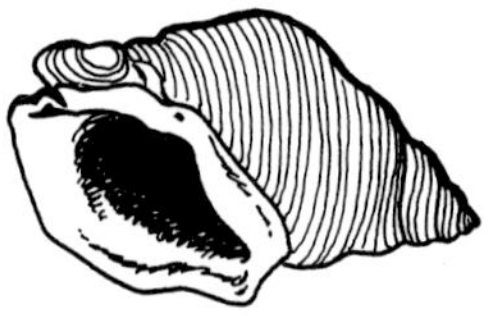

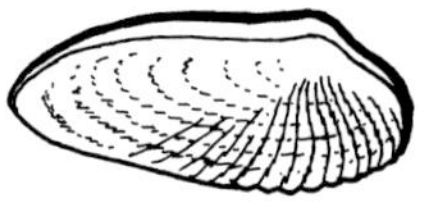
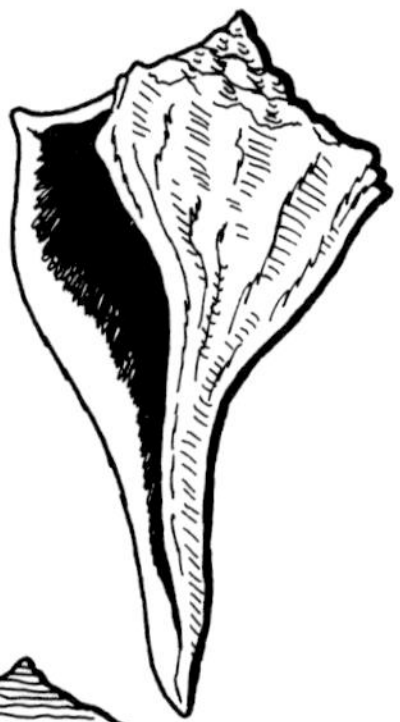
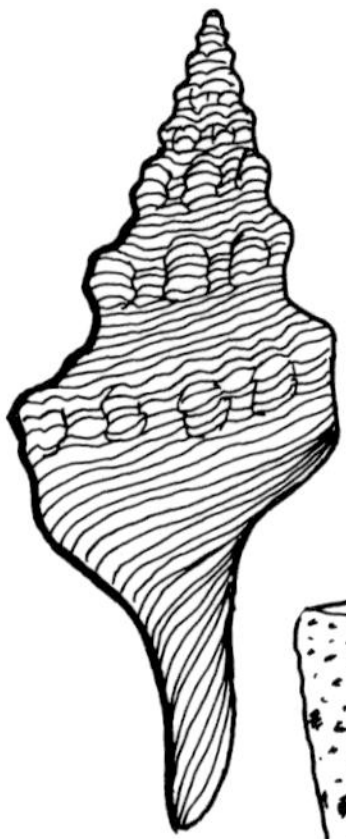
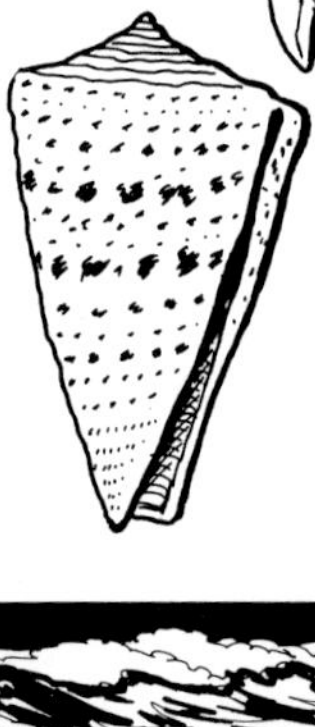

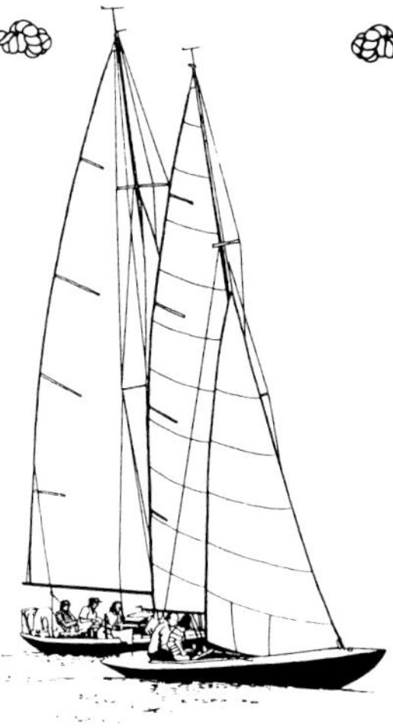

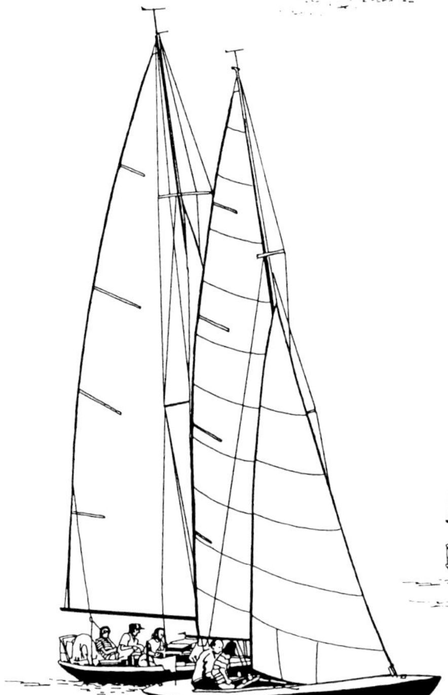

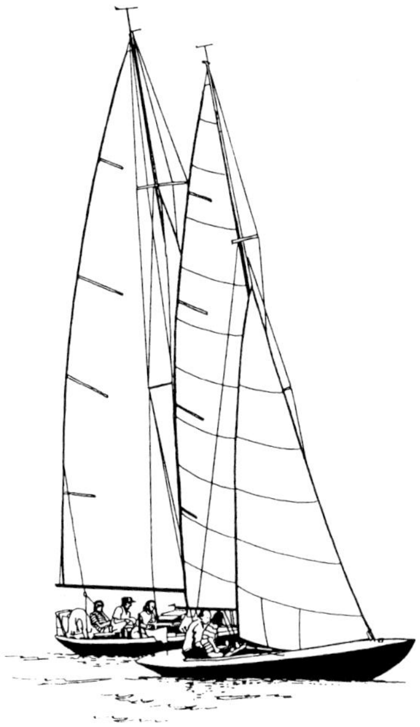

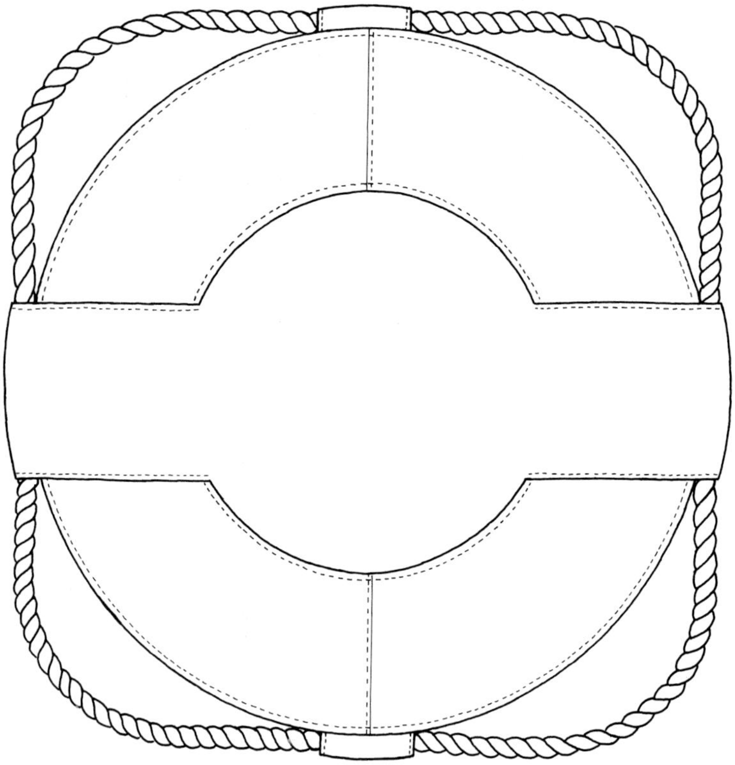

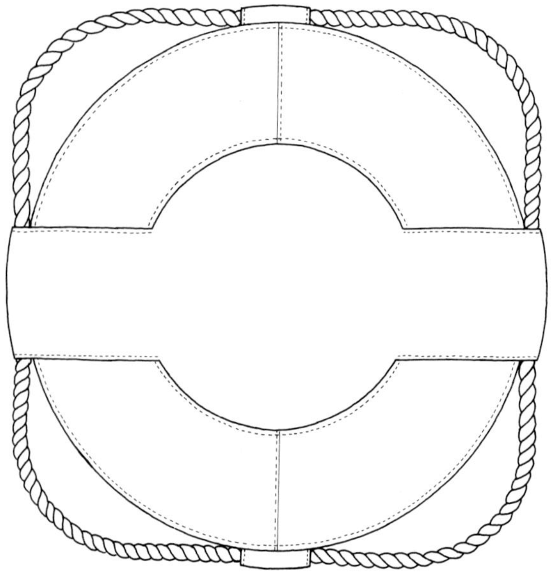

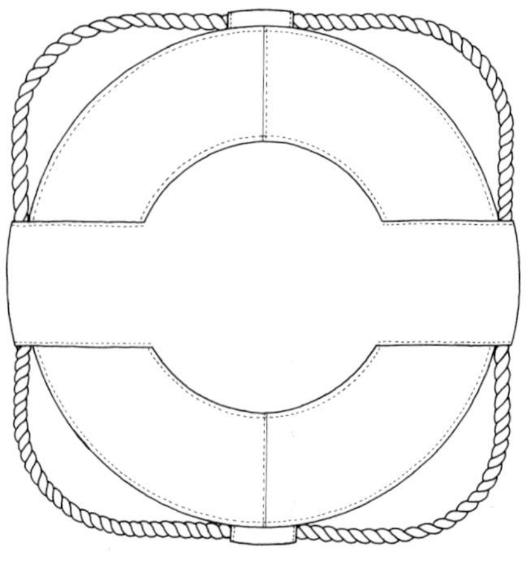